UNSUNG HERO # LALA HARDAYAL JI

INDIA'S FREEDOM STRUGGLE

RIDHI MANGLA

I dedicate this book to all the freedom fighters,
our heroes, who fought for the freedom of India.

Contents

Foreword

"Lala Hardayal Ji"
"Little Angel" as a call Riddhi, is my granddaughter (daughter's daughter). Riddhi has been born different, is acquiring difference, and will be different in life.

Orators and authors have received the greatest attention and position in the world. May it be Swami Vivekanand, Subha Chander Bose, PM Modi or Chetan Bhagat. My "little angle" is a writer. Her Two story books by the name ZUNO & JASMIN have already been published. She published the first in January 2021, the second in January 2022, and the latest one on the day of AMRIT MAHOTSAV.
A few days ago she asked me to suggest the subject of a book. I suggested that she should write on the theme.

"And how can a man die better than facing fearful odds?
For the ashes of his father's and the temples of his Gods".
I suggest to her the name of a forgotten freedom fighter Lala Hardayal Ji and she requested me to write the foreword for the book as she came to know about Lala Hardayal Ji through me.

This small book gives an interesting overall glimpse of a forgotten great hero of the freedom era. I am sure this book will find a respectable response in the minds and hearts of literary people.

I wish my " Little Angle" all success in life.
Jk Gupta

Preface

"Freedom... to live free...is a dream of every creature on this Earth."

It is just because of the spirit of several freedom fighters that we are enjoying freedom. It's all because of them. We all are flying like a free birds just because of their hard work and struggle. You know they all had to face different struggles and troubles to create an independent India.

In this story, I have tried to throw some light on the life of Lala Hardayal Ji.

He was intelligent, sincere, dedicated, hardworking...always dreamt of a free India. How he was blessed with two brains...?

How does he chase his dream...?

Let us peep into his life...so turn the pages and unlock the wealth of his actions and learn from his experiences.

Happy Reading.

Ridhi Mangla

Gangtok

15 August 2022

Acknowledgements

I am thankful to my Nanaji, Sh J. k. Gupta, to help me learn about Lala Hardaya Ji.

It is because of his efforts and guidance that I could pen down some glimpses from the life of this brave Indian Hero.

CHAPTER ONE

VACATION TIME

Spring is going on...What a beautiful day it is....The weather is not so cold nor too hot...Just as simple as it can be...Very pleasant. Cherry blossom is blooming with lovely flowers.

The blackbird is singing melodiously... motivating me to wake up early and do my chores...Just like every day.

I finally forced myself to become an early bird and start the first day of my summer vacation. I woke up from my bed, got ready, and wore my favorite multicolored skirt and cream top. My nose filled up with the delicious pancake smell. Of course my favorite "BREAKFAST"...

I went downstairs and right towards the dining table...My Dad, Mumma, and my elder sister were sitting at the dining table and waiting for me...I sat down on the chair on the left having my sister sitting right beside me. My Mumma, dad, and my sister broke the silence...and started chit-chatting.

Dad started the talk in a little mischievous way...

"Why is everyone so silent here? I wanted to share something...But if you all don't want to listen or even discuss....Then it's your loss...It's something really interesting and amazing...Your choice!"

I and my sister became excited and eager to know what dad wants to share with us...So together we exclaimed, "Dad Don't like that. Share with us please..we want to know what you have to share with all of us...We both are eager to know about it.."

Dad laughed and replied, "Hahaha!! Okay!... See. yesterday, at my office... we were having a fun time after the lunch break. Everyone started asking riddles...And that too all together...No one was waiting for the other to finish...Just kept on talking as if everyone else is listening...

My boss got exhausted and finally screamed and said that "I am not Lala Hardayal! Who can listen to many people at a time..And also I am not having Two - Brains!!"...Everyone got shocked and become silent in the meeting.."

"Now Let's come to the point...I hope you heard my words. Are you all not excited to know about Lala Hardayal ...As from my discussion...You might have heard the word "Two Brains" Right??"

I replied "Yes of course. We heard it. I am eager to know what is "Two
Brains..." And Did Lala Hardayal has Two - Two Brains!!??"

"Well. Yes, He had Two Two Brains. And many different incidents flash out the presence of 2 brains in him.." Dad replied.

"So.."I said by completing my breakfast and drinking a sip of water... "Will you be telling us about those incidents?"

"Ummmm...I could have ...But.I think your Nanaji, will be able to explain to you about Lala Hardayal in a much better way than me..." Dad replied.

"Hmmm...OK...I'll surely question Nanaji. I am really curious to know about him.." I replied with a little smile.

The next day, as my summer vacation is going on..we planned to surprise Nani by visiting her house and having some fun wi

CHAPTER TWO

HAPPINESS HAS NO BOUNDARIES

The covid pandemic emerged from nowhere and hence to prevent it from spreading, a complete lockdown was declared...

We all had to change our plan and postpone it. We had to stay at home. Everyone in the house got disappointed. I was also sad and disheartened. But it was for our good only. I decided to encourage everyone and make them happy, cheerful, and joyous. I also wanted to recharge their batteries and make them energized once again.

I went to the study room..where everyone was sitting. I cheered,

"Hocus Pocus, I have a surprise!! Who wants it???!!"

"I want it", Everyone screamed with happiness.

That was the smile I wished for.

"Ok, the surprise is that......" I continued, with an incomplete sentence. "What??? Complete it, dear".

"Well...The surprise is... we can make a video call to all the cousins, relatives and especially Nanaji and Nani...Isn't it a brilliant idea??" I asked with excitement.

Everyone's excited faces and curiosity vanished. But immediately all charged up again with smiles. All were happy..and overjoyed.

In the evening, We did a video call to my cousins and the whole family.

Everyone was chit-chatting and enjoying. We were playing Damsharaj, and Antakshari, and also everyone was sharing their latest drawings, crafts, dance videos, songs, and other such things...I too showed my artwork...

There was a cheerful noise of gossips, chitter-chatters, and jokes.

Everyone was happy. We all forgot about the lockdown. and we're enjoying every moment of it.

Really happiness has no boundaries.

CHAPTER THREE

NANU'S VIDEO CALL

The next day, I started my day with the chirping of birds and woke up...I got ready and dressed up, I went downstairs, ate my breakfast, did some chit-chat with mom and dad, and then as usual helped Mumma with the dishes and helped her to set the beds and other chores.

Then I went upstairs, sat down on my study table near the window...and started completing my Holidays HomeWork...After some time I felt tired and started thinking about yesterday...from the beginning ...I remembered about the discussion with dad..also about 'The Two Brain Man'

I soon started to imagine a figure of Lala Hardayal. I thought he might be a good observer and intelligent.
I then got curious to know more and more about him.

I quickly completed my Homework..and hurriedly went downstairs...And had a straight look at the clock ....the time was ... 2:00 in the noon....
The time was running faster, and faster. Soon our time for Daily Nanu's Video Call came. The time was already 5:00 ...I got ready as soon as I could and I clicked the icon on the

Family Group for doing a video call...Soon everyone was in the video call ..but....Nanu was facing net issues..and said that he'll join after some time...
Till that time everyone started talking chatting with each other...I was silent and the thought of the two-brain man was prevailing in my mind and I wasn't in a mood to talk to anyone ...

When Nanu joined the video call...he asked, "Why was I so silent....I told him that “Nanu...I wanted a favor from you. Will you help me?”

Nanu replied, “ Yes Yes,...Tell me what happened. ”

I said “Nanu...My dad told me that Lala Hardayal had 2 brains...From that time I m thinking about it...Could You please tell me something related to him...I am curious to know...”

Nanu replied, “ Yes Of Course dear...I hope your cousins and everyone else is also excited..”

All my cousins exclaimed with excitement, “Yes Nanu..We are eager to know..Please tell us..Please Nanu..Please”.

“Okay Then...Everyone tighten your seat belts and get ready for a small adventure to The World of Lala Hardayal Ji...” Nanu said with a little happiness.

“Lala Hadarayal was born in Punjab, during the British rule, on 14 October 1884...He was a freedom fighter, an unsung hero. You may not find anything about him in your textbooks. He was not much recognized but he did a lot for India's Freedom...During his time...
Britishers didn't allow Indians to get educated...Hence Lala Hardayal took much more attention to educating the people of India. He had indeed two brains. No one could match the intelligence he possessed ” Nanu continued.

"Rest..I'll tell you all in the next Video Call...Will that be okay? I hope that you all are feeling more and more excited...Aren't you???"

"Yes, Nanu...We are all curious ...Thank you so much for telling us about him.." We all replied.

"Okay then... Let's meet tomorrow, then I'll tell you more about Lala Hardayal", Nanu ended the video call.

CHAPTER FOUR

BOY WITH MAGICAL TWO BRAINS

It was a beautiful morning. The sky was full of clouds. Clouds were running here and there. A cold breeze was filling all with freshness.

As always there was no change in my routine.

You know...The time passes fast. Today I completed my Hindi holiday homework. I complete all necessary tasks by 4:00 PM. After that, it was time to take some rest.

At 5:00 it's our Nanu's video call time. I am excited about today's call...As Nanu'll be explaining about Lala Hardayal in detail. I know he explains everything easily, in a short, crisp, and engaging manner.

And that's it...It's 5:00 ..Oh...Nanu's call is ringing already...

I hurriedly joined the call. But I found out that Nanu was having a bad network connection..and hence was joining and leaving again and again. He was waiting for a proper net.

Till then I and my cousins started thinking about Lala

Hardayal.

I said, “I am really curious about Lala Hardayal and his experiences being a freedom fighter. He might have faced several obstacles and issues, and I think no one even encouraged him to fight for freedom. All these could have disappointed, and discouraged Lala Hardayal. He was courageous and fought for India.”

My cousin Pihu said “Yes...It might have been very tough...Especially, there was a lack of resources and support.”

Now...Nanu’s Net stopped fluctuating and he joined the meeting.

Nanu started the talk. “Hey Hey Hey...Have you all thought a little about Lala Hardayal.??”

“Yes, Nanu. We were discussing him only” I said.

“Oh, that’s nice...Shall I explain in detail..and clear all your doubts..?”Nanu asked

“Yes... yes, Nanu...Pl continue..” We all cheered.

Nanu started... “Ok. As from my past discussion with you all. Today I’ll be telling you about some incidents that happened with Lala Hardayal...It’s gonna be fun...You’ll enjoy it...Let me start with his childhood. I think at that time he was in class 5 or 6...”

“He was in his school. His Science teacher was teaching the class about how nutrition in animals takes place. It was a bit difficult topic to understand. Hardayal was sitting at a desk, near the window. He looked outside and found that a few women were singing and carrying a pot full of water. They were singing some patriotic songs. Hardayal liked the song very much. Suddenly, chalk hit his hand. It was thrown at him by his teacher. His teacher was very angry.

He asked, ‘Hardayal... What are you doing? Where is your concentration? What are you looking at? Get up and get out of my class.'

Lala Hardayal was a person of truth. He replied, 'Teacher. I was looking at the women carrying pots of water. Their music and lyrics attracted me towards them...'

The teacher became angry and shouted, "Oh Lyrics... they are singing in a low voice and still you could hear their lyrics...Tell me what was I taught in class?'

Lala Hardayal explained everything pointwise to the teacher, exactly the way the teacher had taught.

The teacher was shocked to listen to him. He explained everything step by step.

How can a boy listen to two things at a time?

To test him further, the teacher further asked him to sing the song which had attracted his attention. Hardayal sang the song also thoroughly.

"Through this incident, one can learn that Lala Hardayal had Two Brains. Isn't it amazing...He didn't even get scolded by the teacher. If we had two brains then it would be so nice. Hahaha", Nanu laughed.

"Nanu...We would be lucky if we have two brains. Because the teacher won't scold us. It would have been really all well and good." I giggled.

There was a box full of laughs and happiness. Everyone cheered. I captured this moment with the help of our always-ready tool. Yes, you got it right... 'Screenshot'. The most useful tool these days is to capture memories sitting inside the house.

Nanu started again, "Now do you all want to know more about the childhood of Hardayal? He was a very sharp boy with a lot of concentration power and his intelligence was unbeatable. His love for the country was unfathomable."

"Yes, Nanu. We always have time for such interesting talks and discussion."

We all exclaimed. We were feeling as if we are living with Hardayal and he is our classmate only.

Nani brought tea and Samosa for Nanu and here my mom brought the same for me. We all enjoyed ourselves as if we are together.

CHAPTER FIVE

Brilliant Student and a Keen Learner

After eating a delicious homemade Samosa, I was curious to know about Hardayal. I was thinking, " What will Nanu share next about him?"

"Hahaha.Okay...Here's another circumstance that happened.."Nanu Continued.

"When Lala Hardayal was in 10th class. He was preparing for the board exams. He was a very intelligent and dedicated student. Very soon he prepared everything and was fully ready for the exam.

On his examination day, he reached the examination hall. The invigilator was a Britisher. He handed over the question paper to everyone. Lala Hardayal completed all the answers on time. He handed over the exam sheets to the examiner."

"After everyone's submission of answer sheets. The examiner started checking the answers. When he came to the answer sheet submitted by

Lala Hardayal.He glanced at the sheets and he was shocked to go through them. He then refused to put marks on that. Authorities got upset over his behavior and we're sure that Hardayal must have written something bad about the British Rule and that's why the teacher had denied putting marks on it. They called the examiner and asked him to write down the reason on the answer sheet so that they can punish the student and teach him a lesson.

The examiner looked down and wrote the reason,

"The Examinee knows better than the examiner. "

Authorities got shocked to know about the unbeatable personality of a young boy.

"Children...You know he did this because Lala Hardayal was brilliant in every term, be from the point of view of language..and he wrote the answers in English in such a way that the examiner was astonished to see an Indian speak and beautifully write English and so perfect. Hence he wrote that reason."

"Ooo..la..la...What an incident...The Britishers who are mostly known for their perfection in English failed in front of an Indian. And they also said that the examinee was much better in English than his teacher. He had a great concentration power," I was very thrilled.

"Unlocking the treasure of history with a bundle of keys is quite tough...But Nanu you are unlocking it with the right key..And because of that, we can know about the history of India's freedom. Thank you so much and...In the next video call pl do tell us about other achievements, appreciations, and other tasks carried out by Lala Hardayal in his life for freedom." I said.

"Hahaha...Let's meet in the next video call...It'll be fun...Hope you enjoyed today's call...And are curious to know about the struggle of Lala Hardayal for freedom... Bye

Bye. " Nanu giggled.

Nanu Ended the video call.

CHAPTER SIX

DEDICATION IS THE ROAD TO SUCCESS

Today evening is very cool. It was raining since morning. The blackbird which used to visit early morning is chirping outside melodiously. It's Time for Nanu's Video Call.

Let's join it and get some more knowledge about Lala Hardayal, he was an extraordinary freedom fighter.

Nanu joined. Everyone was ready in the meeting room. Ha! Ha! Ha!
Digital World's Meeting Room. Everybody was excited.

Nanu started. "Hello, Curious Kids...Let's start with a new incident and story...I'm so happy to see that you are keen to learn about Lala Hardayal. I'm sure you will learn many lessons from his life and will fill with new energy to deal with situations," Nanu Continued.

"Today I'll be telling you all about Lala Hardayal's Family Life...His family was financially sound. His father Gauri Dayal Mathur was a

District Court Reader. He always wanted his son to get proper education and excel in his studies. His mother Bholi Rani was a very sweet, polite & motivating lady. Everyone knows the importance of education, especially during British Rule. So that's about Lala

Hardayal's family. Lala Hardayal was keen to get higher education so that he could contribute to Freedom Movement."

"Lala Hardayal studied at Cambridge School & he completed his graduation from St.Stephen College, Delhi. His love for education moved him again to Punjab, where he completed his Master's. He was the University topper and till today, no one could beat his records in the study...The British Government could not ignore his potential and he got a scholarship for higher studies at Oxford University. Isn't it amazing??"

"Yes, Nanu...Getting an opportunity to study in such different and famous schools is extraordinary...Wow.." I replied.

"Hmm...Education is the key to Success...Let me share one more incident from that time 'The Indian Civil Services Examination for

Administrative services were conducted only in London, not in India. " Nanu continued.

"Kids, do you know...This exam was necessary to attain a higher position in Indian Administration, and Britishers conduct it in London.

Many Indians were not in the position to visit London and appear for that, in that way only Britishers were able to get through that and they can continue their Rule over Indian."

"Lala Hardayal had a clear vision that to change the conditions of people, one needs to be a part of the administration."

"Lala Hardayal prepared for ICS...cleared the examination...Two students scored the same marks i.e. Lala Hardayal & A British girl.

After the written exam, it was time for a Personal Interview. Everyone knew that they will disqualify Hardayal.

A committee was all set to conduct an Interview.

They asked some questions and both students qualified that also with the same score. The situation was getting bitter. The committee could not get a chance to disqualify Hardayal, rather all were appreciating his knowledge.
Lastly, one committee judge comes up with a solution for the selection of the final candidate.

Both candidates were given a book and one day to learn the book. The final question-answer session was decided to be conducted from the book. Lala Hardayal learned it properly.

The next day, despite questions, both were asked to tell the text from the book. Both were able to tell the contents of the book thoroughly. Again the committee was in dilemma. By that time, this case has become a piece of front-page news and people were keen to know the outcome. So the British government too was under stress.

All were confused. At that time Lala Hardayal asked to share his idea to complete the selection process. He suggested that now both of us can explain the content of the book starting from the end to the start.

Committee found that perfect as they don't have any other solution, and was bearing tremendous pressure for fair judgment.

The British girl failed in that task. But Lala Hardayal explained the entire content in reverse order too with precision."

“See...Lala Hardayal was so good at learning and memorizing things. This shows that Lala Hardayal was a wonderful learner and a keen observer. He passed the exam with dedication and hard work. His memory was just superb. From this incident, we got to know that you can achieve your dreams if you pay full attention and have decided to get that. Through Hard work only we can accomplish our dream and desires... So kids Set your Goal, work towards it and achieve that,” Nanu said.

“Yes. Thank you so much..for giving us such a lesson related to hard work..from now on we pledge to do hard work and fulfill our goals,” I replied.

Nanu smiled..and ended the video call.

CHAPTER SEVEN

PARTY WITH BOILED POTATOES

In the evening, when we combine Juice & Bun with Nanu's video call ... tastes amazing and becomes yummyiliciuos ...When Nanu shares the stories and incidents of Lala Hardayal, it gets more and more interesting to eat the Buns.

Let us join the Meeting. Nanu must be waiting...today throughout the day my mind was thinking about Lala Hardayal. He was so knowledgeable.

"Ho! ho! ho!... Let's start the meeting...Today I'll be sharing how Lala Hardayal fought for India,...And how he has trodden the path of becoming revolutionary and a freedom fighter," Nanu continued.

"Lala Hardayal was a freedom fighter...He believed in simple living and hence he left the Indian Civil Service career, He was an intellectual person. He was a source of inspiration for many. He inspired many Indians who were living in Canada, US, who initiated campaigns against BRITSH RULE IN INDIA and their unjust practices..."

"Since childhood... He was influenced by Arya Samaj...He was sharing his views on the value of freedom in various newspapers and magazines. Once Lala Hardayal wrote 'our object is not to reform the government, but to RE-FORM it ...' This made the British govt. upset and he was put under surveillance by police. Then he decided to leave his ICS career and & returned to India so that he could make his dream of Free India a reality."

"Nanu...It's a nice opportunity for all of us kids. Because ...Your stories and incidents when mixed up with Buns ..become more interesting.." I replied while eating a bun with juice.

"Ohh...So you are eating buns...Delicious...Enjoy...But do you know what Lala Hardayal liked to eat..As I said...Lala Hardayal focused on living a simple life...He ate only boiled vegetables and potatoes...Let me share one more incident, it was indeed a funny one..."Nanu continued.

"Lala Hardayal was teaching at University. Many students become his followers. He was a great source of inspiration for them. One day some students who were inspired by Lala Hardayal were coming to visit him on his birthday...They were expecting a party of delicious food...But...There was a shock waiting for them..."

"Lala Hardayal was presenting the food on the dining table...All the students were shocked to see boiled vegetables and potatoes on the table despite their expectations.."Nanu continued. They also found that there was no bed and Lala Ji used to sleep on the floor on a thin mattress.

"This incident showed that Lala Hardayal was a simple living person..who wore simple clothes, simple food i.e boiled food, and simple speaking style.."

"Hence we should be simple and try our best in everything

even if it goes a little out of track...If something wrong happens then just say all is good..and give it a fresh start.

Also...we should enjoy every moment...We shouldn't lose hope...If something unexpected is happening..then something good will also happen...as you know every cloud has a silver lining...So keep hope alive in your heart and enjoy and always do your best..." Nanu said. "Yes, We surely will. Thank you once again...what a great and inspirational personality Lala Hardayal was. ," I replied.

Nanu smiled..and the video call ended for the day.

CHAPTER EIGHT

PEN IS A POWERFUL WEAPON

Wow...How delicious french fries are... especially with Piri Piri...I love them...What nice weather it is...Cloudy as well as Sunny...Sometimes it's raining, sometimes it's cloudy and even sunny...Magical Nature.

It's 5 already...Let us join in on an adventure with Nanu...on a virtual track.

Nanu Joined and said, "Hello kids...Excited today??"

"Yes, Nanu. I am rather more excited than yesterday... I am curious to know about his struggle to fight for freedom..." I replied.

Pihu was very excited, she shared that she has finished her holiday homework. "Now, what should I do?" Pihu asked.

"Oh! It is a very good thing that you have done your work on time. So... now you can use your time for extra activities...you can read books...even write stories...Lala Hardayal was very fond of reading and writing." Nanu replied. He was trying his best to keep us happy. As he knew that we were missing being together because of lockdown.

"Ok...today I'll share a little more about the freedom struggle of Lala Hardayal."Nanu continued.

"In India...Lala Hardayal had started writing articles in newspapers...All his writings were eye-openers...The public started following him in huge numbers. Due to his increasing popularity and impact, the British Government got fed up and banned his writings.."Nanu said.

"Nanu...What is the meaning of a ban...Pl explain.."I asked.

"It means...Now no newspaper publishers can publish Lala Hardayal's works, ideas, and articles.."Nanu replied.

"Oh! his words were so powerful.."I thought.

"Ok...But as we know one cannot stop a dedicated person...At this moment Lala Hardayal started his own News Daily..but the British government was chasing him like anything and were determined to stop him by any means," Nanu continued.

"Lala Lajpat Rai who was a mentor of Lala Hardayal suggested that he should leave India ..Haradayal followed the instructions and moved to various countries and continued his work of spreading his ideas about the Free India Movement...His followers were increasing day by day..." Nanu said.

"Even though he was the fountain of inspiration of many...He slept on the floor...One more thing that he believed in was the practice of Yoga and Meditation... People thought that Lala Hardayal was physically active & mentally strong just because of Yoga and meditation... Lala Hardayal said..'These are the food for my Body and Brain..'"

" He was down to Earth...He used to read books whenever he found time...He also wrote many books...He started teaching at various universities...All his students were fond of his ideology...Ultimately, Because of Lala Hardayal's success and progress, the British forced him to resign from his job at University... But he remained a source to motivate people to fight for Free India Movement," Nanu said.

"Children, you know...Knowledge has no boundaries...We should be ready to put some knowledge in our bags of thoughts and ideas...That's it...We should inspire others and also take inspiration inspired from others...You should feel lucky that you are receiving some knowledge from a person." Nanu said.

"Yes, Nanu...Thank you. We all feel lucky to obtain knowledge from you about Lala Hardayal. You are our true inspiration. Thank you so much, Nanu...Keep inspiring us...And also..please keep sharing such incidents about other unsung heroes who fought for our freedom but were never given some recognition, praise, and appreciation for their sacrifice, and hard work.." I replied.

"Hahaha...I am really happy that you are loving the incidents that I chatted about...And yes..surely...after Lala Hardayal we can chat about some other unsung hero. India is a land of brave soldiers who had served the nation without failure. I'll share details about other freedom fighters too.

You encouraged me a lot. I am so happy to see that all my little flowers are blooming with the energy to learn from great personalities. God bless you all. I thank you too for motivating me to unlock the treasure of the past... it was lying inside the treasure trunk of mine.." Nanu replied with a smile and ended the video call.

CHAPTER NINE

FREE INDIA # DREAM OF FREEDOM FIGHTERS

Time for Nanu's video call.

"Nanu...Please tell us more about Lala Hardayal..." I asked.

"You know...as I said last time...we must try to give some recognition to the unknown and unsung freedom fighters...Most of the people didn't know about Lala Hardayal and his sacrifice...but...you know it right?...so...share it with many others...and inspire them...motivate them and encourage them. In this way, you could understand the value of freedom, and you, we all are enjoying it.

So many had the dream of Free India...and they consistently worked to make their dream come true. We

have to pay respect to them and share their stories to keep the unsung heroes alive. Try your best."
Nanu said.

"And also you all should be grateful to all the freedom fighters who fought for the country's freedom and wanted the country to gradually develop and change. You are flying like a free bird just because of your hard work and struggle. You know they all had to face different struggles and troubles to create an independent India," Nanu continued.

"Yes, Nanu we all are glad to know that it's their tireless work because of which we threw the gates of the cage made by the Britishers open and flew away...We are thankful to all the unsung heroes.."I replied with a gracious look..and a beautiful smile. I was feeling like a proud person.

Nanu smiled, " Now, we all should meet on the next vacation. Lockdown would be over by then, okay, so plan your trip...bye for now," and the video call ended.

CHAPTER TEN

PROUD TO BE AN INDIAN

My vacation is over. This year because of a lockdown, we could not visit my grandmother's house. But everything happens for a good reason. My cousins and I enjoyed it a lot and had great fun together.

We came to know about the period when India was under British Rule. It is just because of the spirit of several freedom fighters that we are enjoying freedom. It's all because of them.

With the help of Nanu..we got to know about Lala Hardayal who struggled a lot for India's freedom. It must have been a difficult task. He faced different opinions of the communities and obstacles created by the British Government. But even after crossing all these bravely, we don't know about him, or his contribution to gaining Independence. Now you know and I too know about him.

So together let's pledge that we'll share the incidents of Lala Hardayal and his struggles.
PROMISE??

Let's give some recognition and pay respect to the unsung heroes and give them a good reason to smile, and be happy forever. I am proud to be a citizen of Free India. Our love for them should never die.

Jai Hind. Jai Bharat.

Lala Hardayal Ji

Jai Hind Jai Bharat

About The Author

The author of the book is Ridhi Mangla. She is a 13 yr old girl, a student of class 8th, Army Public School, Gangtok. She is an avid reader and her inclination toward books and great Indian Heros made her write the story of Lala Hardayal Ji. Earlier she published a series of two storybooks for children by the name "Zuno And Jasmine". She is fond of coding and creating animations.

Ridhi Mangla

About The Author

Previous Works

First Book

Second Book

9 798887 834412

Printed by Libri Plureos GmbH in Hamburg,
Germany